Dear Parents,

Thank you for choosing our cursive handwriting practice book to help your child develop beautiful and confident handwriting skills. This book is designed specifically for young learners aged 6-8 and provides a fun, engaging, and structured approach to learning cursive writing.

<u>How to Use This Book</u>

Each cursive letter of the alphabet is practiced across four pages, ensuring thorough learning and gradual skill development.

1st Page: Introduction to the Letter

- The letter is introduced with arrows indicating the correct formation.
- Ample tracing practice for both uppercase and lowercase letters.
- Tracing starts with larger letters and gradually decreases in size to build fine motor skills and control.

2nd Page: Transition from Tracing to Writing

- Your child will start writing the letter on their own.
- Similar to the first page, the letter size decreases gradually to enhance precision and confidence.

3rd Page: Fun Coloring and Tracing

- Combining creativity with practice: Your child can color a cute animal illustration related to the letter.

4th Page: Writing the letter within the context of a word

- On this page your child will practice how to join letters correctly.
- Letters that have not been introduced yet are in a normal font, while letters that have been learned are in a dotted format for tracing.

Additional Practice:
At the end of the book, you will find six pages dedicated to practicing sentences, helping your child apply their cursive writing skills in a fun and meaningful way.

Happy Learning!
Andrea from Joyful Learning™

ABCDEFGHIJKLMNOPQRSTUVWXYZ

a b c d e f g h i j k l m n o p q r s t u v w x y z

Let's color!

Ant

Sight Words with A & a

about about about

after after after

all all all

am am am am

Ant Ant Ant Ant

a b c d e f g h i j k l m n o p q r s t u v w x y z

$\mathcal{B}$ $\mathcal{B}$ $\mathcal{B}$ $\mathcal{B}$ $\mathcal{B}$

$\mathcal{B}$ $\mathcal{B}$ $\mathcal{B}$ $\mathcal{B}$

$\mathcal{B}$ $\mathcal{B}$ $\mathcal{B}$ $\mathcal{B}$ $\mathcal{B}$ $\mathcal{B}$ $\mathcal{B}$

$\mathcal{B}$ $\mathcal{B}$ $\mathcal{B}$ $\mathcal{B}$ $\mathcal{B}$ $\mathcal{B}$ $\mathcal{B}$ $\mathcal{B}$

$\mathcal{h}$ $\mathcal{h}$ $\mathcal{h}$ $\mathcal{h}$

$\mathcal{h}$ $\mathcal{h}$ $\mathcal{h}$ $\mathcal{h}$

$\mathcal{h}$ $\mathcal{h}$ $\mathcal{h}$ $\mathcal{h}$ $\mathcal{h}$ $\mathcal{h}$ $\mathcal{h}$ $\mathcal{h}$

$\mathcal{h}$ $\mathcal{h}$ $\mathcal{h}$ $\mathcal{h}$ $\mathcal{h}$ $\mathcal{h}$ $\mathcal{h}$ $\mathcal{h}$

$\mathcal{A}$ $\mathcal{B}$ $\mathcal{C}$ $\mathcal{D}$ $\mathcal{E}$ $\mathcal{F}$ $\mathcal{G}$ $\mathcal{H}$ $\mathcal{I}$ $\mathcal{J}$ $\mathcal{K}$ $\mathcal{L}$ $\mathcal{M}$ $\mathcal{N}$ $\mathcal{O}$ $\mathcal{P}$ $\mathcal{Q}$ $\mathcal{R}$ $\mathcal{S}$ $\mathcal{T}$ $\mathcal{U}$ $\mathcal{V}$ $\mathcal{W}$ $\mathcal{X}$ $\mathcal{Y}$ $\mathcal{Z}$

a b c d e f g h i j k l m n o p q r s t u v w x y z

Let's color!

Bee

Sight Words with B & b

be be be be be be be be be

been been been

by by by by by by

been been been

Bee Bee Bee Bee Bee

Fun Fact:

Bees communicate with each other by dancing. They use a "waggle dance" to show other bees where to find food.

a b c d e f g h i j k l m n o p q r s t u v w x y z

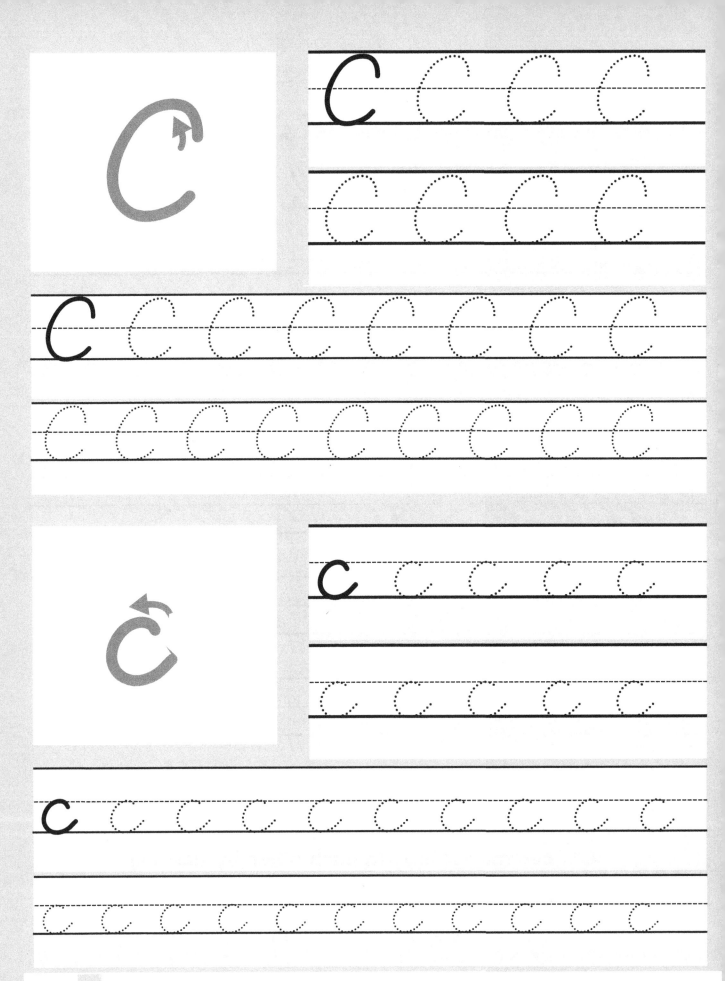

a b c d e f g h i j k l m n o p q r s t u v w x y z

Let's color!

Camel

Sight Words with
C & c

an an an an an

ome ome ome

ould ould ould

ar ar ar ar ar

Camel Camel

Fun Fact:
Camels are known as the "ships of the desert" because they are perfectly adapted to life in the desert. They can go for weeks without water, and when they do drink, they can consume up to 40 gallons in one go. Their humps store fat, which they can convert into water when needed.

a b c d e f g h i j k l m n o p q r s t u v w x y z

D

D D D D D D D D D D D D D D D D D D D

d

d d d d d d d d d d d d d d d d d d d d d d d d d d d d d d

A B C D E F G H I J K L M N O P Q R S T U V W X Y Z

a b c d e f g h i j k l m n o p q r s t u v w x y z

Let's color!

Dolphin

Sight Words with D & d

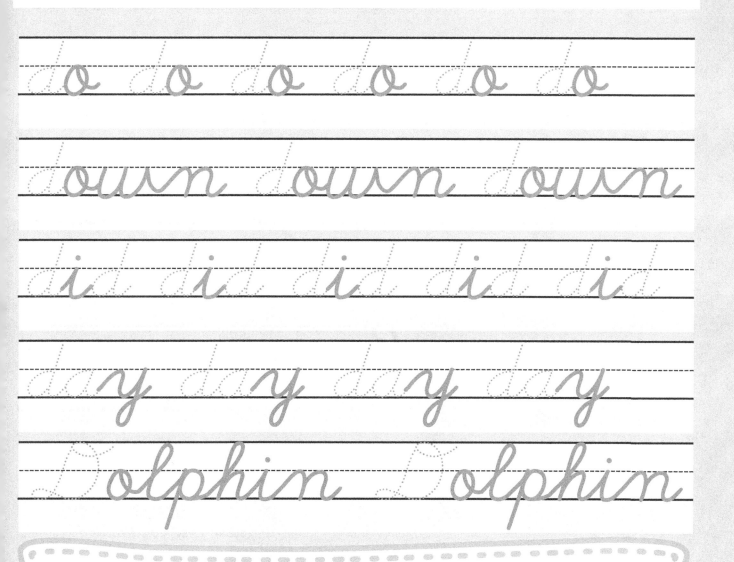

do do do do do do do

down down down

di di di di di di

day day day day day day

Dolphin Dolphin

Fun Fact:
Dolphins are very intelligent and can recognize
themselves in a mirror.

a b c d e f g h i j k l m n o p q r s t u v w x y z

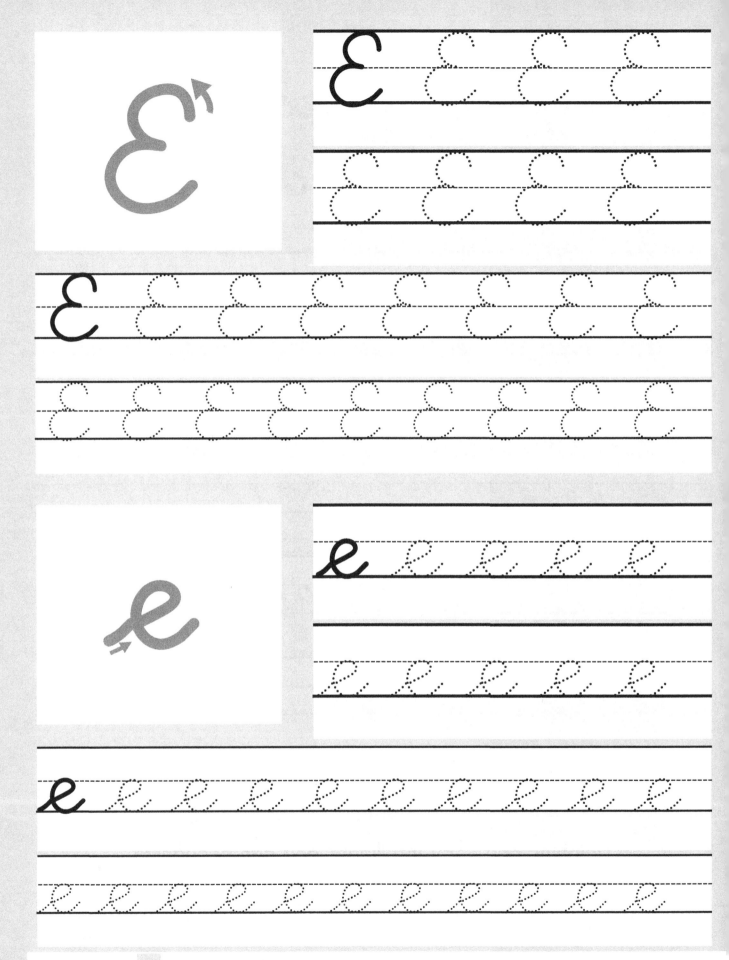

abcde**f**ghijklmnopqrstuvwxyz

Sight Words with E&e

h   h   h   h

r   r   r   r

ight   ight   ight

y   y   y   y   y

e ph nt   e ph nt

Fun Fact:

Elephants are the largest land animals. Their trunks have over 40,000 muscles and can be used to pick up tiny objects.

a b c d e f g h i j k l m n o p q r s t u v w x y z

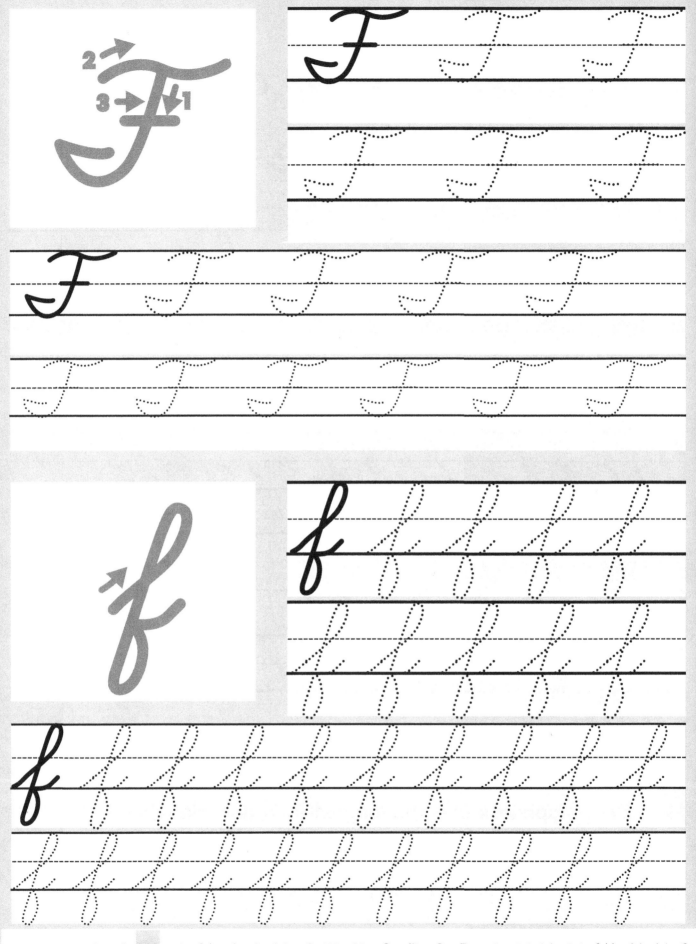

A B C D E F G H I J K L M N O P 2 R S T U V W X Y Z

a b c d e f g h i j k l m n o p q r s t u v w x y z

Let's color!

Frog

Sight Words with F & f

for for for for for

find find find

from from from

friend friend

frog frog frog

Fun Fact:

Frogs can breathe through their skin as well as their lungs.

a b c d e f g h i j k l m n o p q r s t u v w x y z

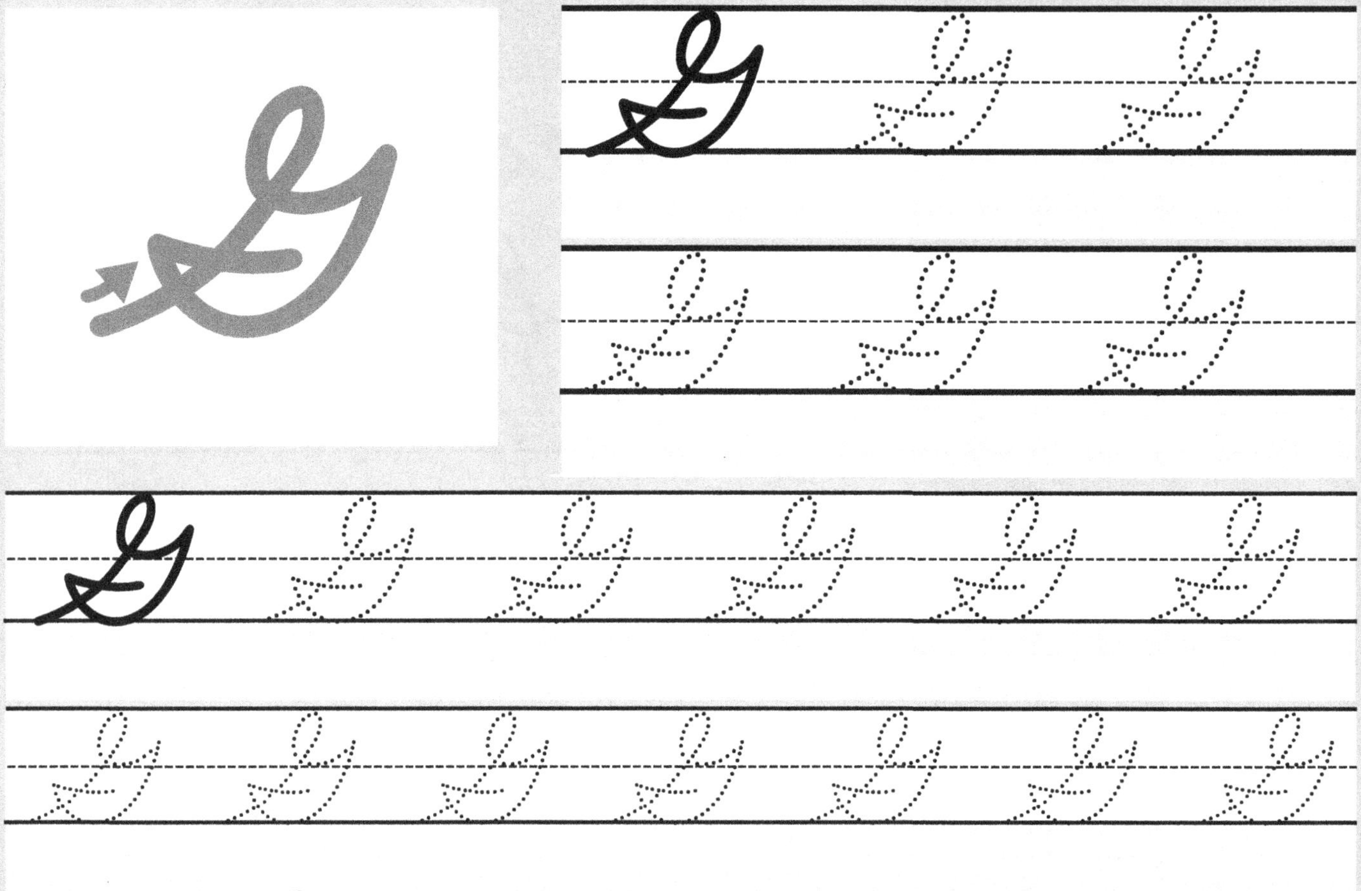

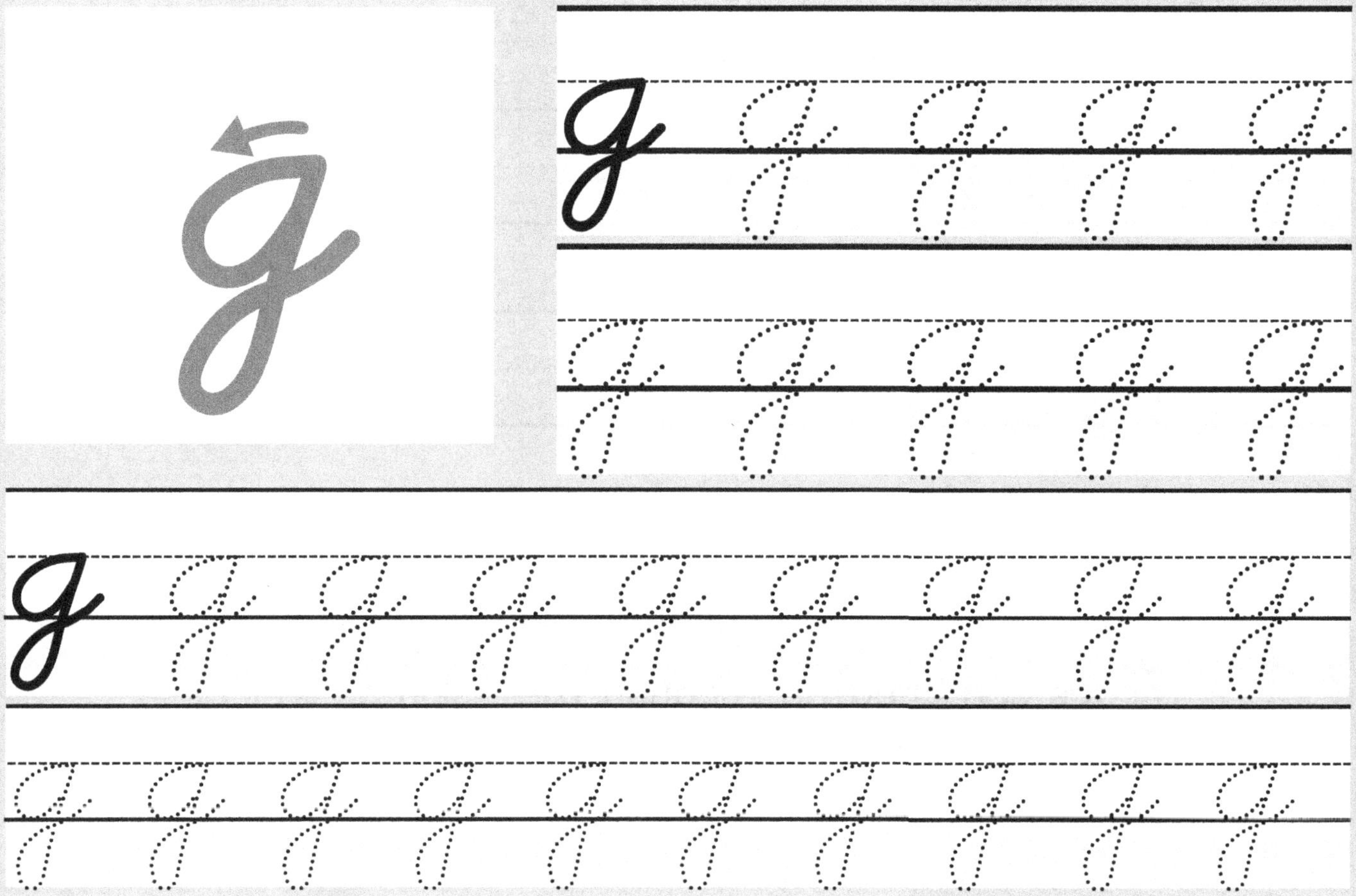

G G G G

G G G G

G G G G G G

G G G G G G G G

g g g g g

g g g g g

g g g g g g g g

g g g g g g g g

abcdef**g**hijklmnopqrstuvwxyz

Let's color!

Giraffe

Sight Words with G & g

go go go go go go go

good good good good

giv giv giv

grt grt grt

Giraffe Giraff

Fun Fact:
Giraffes have the same number of neck bones as
humans—just seven—but theirs are much longer!

a b c d e f g h i j k l m n o p q r s t u v w x y z

a b c d e f g h i j k l m n o p q r s t u v w x y z

Let's color!

Hedgehog

Sight Words with
H & h

he he he he he he he

hou hou hou

her her her her her

hour hour hour hour hour

Hedgehog Hedgehog

Fun Fact:
Hedgehogs are known for their unique defense mechanism of rolling into a tight ball, with their spines sticking out to protect themselves from predators. They can have up to 7,000 spines on their back.

a b c d e f g h i j k l m n o p q r s t u v w x y z

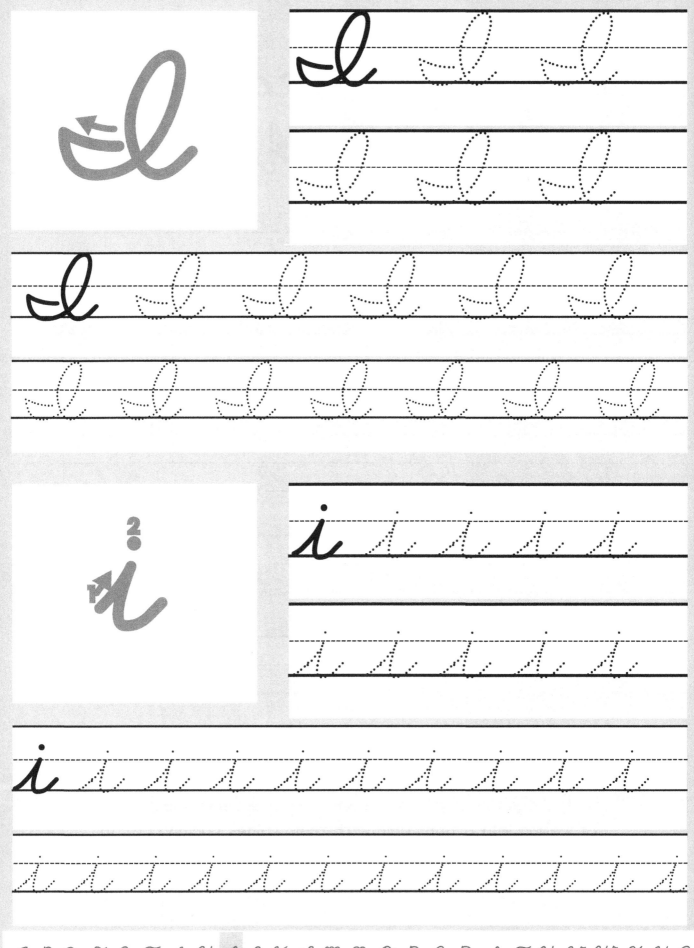

a b c d e f g h i j k l m n o p q r s t u v w x y z

Let's color!

Iguana

Sight Words with I & i

in in in in in in in

s s s s s s s s

t t t t t t t t

into into into

Iguana Iguana

Fun Fact:
An iguana can hold its breath for up to 30 minutes.

a b c d e f g h i j k l m n o p q r s t u v w x y z

a b c d e f g h i j k l m n o p q r s t u v w x y z

Let's color!

Jellyfish

Sight Words with J & j

joy joy joy joy joy

just just just just

jump jump jump

joh joh joh joh joh joh

jellyfish jellyfish

Fun Fact:
Jellyfish don't have brains, hearts, or bones. They
have been around for over 500 million years!

a b c d e f g h i j k l m n o p q r s t u v w x y z

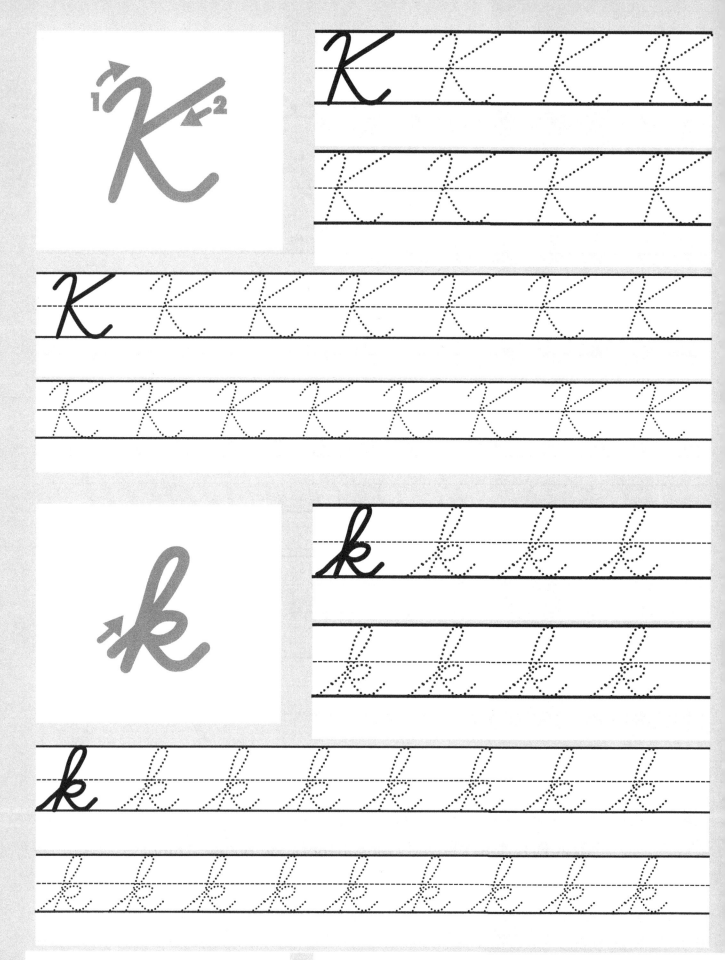

K K K K K

K K

K K

K

k k k k k k k

k k

k k

k

a b c d e f g h i j k l m n o p q r s t u v w x y z

Let's color!

Kangaroo

Sight Words with K & k

kind kind kind kind

know know know know

keep p keep p keep p keep p

king king king king

Kangaroo Kangaroo

Fun Fact:

Kangaroos can't walk backwards. They use their powerful legs to jump around.

a b c d e f g h i j k l m n o p q r s t u v w x y z

$\mathcal{L}$ $\mathcal{L}$ $\mathcal{L}$ $\mathcal{L}$

$\mathcal{L}$ $\mathcal{L}$ $\mathcal{L}$ $\mathcal{L}$

$\mathcal{L}$ $\mathcal{L}$ $\mathcal{L}$ $\mathcal{L}$ $\mathcal{L}$ $\mathcal{L}$

$\mathcal{L}$ $\mathcal{L}$ $\mathcal{L}$ $\mathcal{L}$ $\mathcal{L}$ $\mathcal{L}$ $\mathcal{L}$

l l l l l

l l l l l

l l l l l l l l l l l

l l l l l l l l l l l

$\mathcal{A}$ $\mathcal{B}$ $\mathcal{C}$ $\mathcal{D}$ $\mathcal{E}$ $\mathcal{F}$ $\mathcal{G}$ $\mathcal{H}$ $\mathcal{I}$ $\mathcal{J}$ $\mathcal{K}$ $\mathcal{L}$ $\mathcal{M}$ $\mathcal{N}$ $\mathcal{O}$ $\mathcal{P}$ $\mathcal{Q}$ $\mathcal{R}$ $\mathcal{S}$ $\mathcal{T}$ $\mathcal{U}$ $\mathcal{V}$ $\mathcal{W}$ $\mathcal{X}$ $\mathcal{Y}$ $\mathcal{Z}$

abcdefghij k l m n o p q r s t u v w x y z

Let's color!

Lion

Sight Words with L & l

like like like like

look look look look

little little little

last last last last

Lion Lion Lion

Fun Fact:
Lions are known as the "king of the jungle," but they actually live in savannas and grasslands.

a b c d e f g h i j k l m n o p q r s t u v w x y z

$\mathcal{M}$

$\mathcal{M}$ $\mathcal{M}$ $\mathcal{M}$

$\mathcal{M}$ $\mathcal{M}$ $\mathcal{M}$

$\mathcal{M}$ $\mathcal{M}$ $\mathcal{M}$ $\mathcal{M}$ $\mathcal{M}$

$\mathcal{M}$ $\mathcal{M}$ $\mathcal{M}$ $\mathcal{M}$ $\mathcal{M}$ $\mathcal{M}$

m

m m m

m m m

m m m m

m m m m m m

A B C D E F G H I J K L **M** N O P 2 R S T U V W X Y Z

m m m m

m m

m m

m

m m m m m m

m m m

m m

m

a b c d e f g h i j k l m n o p q r s t u v w x y z

Let's color!

Monkey

Sight Words with M & m

me me me me me me me

my my my my my

much much much much

many many many many

monkey monkey

Fun Fact:
A group of monkeys is called a troop. Some troops can have as many as 500 members.

a b c d e f g h i j k l m n o p q r s t u v w x y z

N n

$\mathcal{N}$ $\mathcal{N}$ $\mathcal{N}$ $\mathcal{N}$ $\mathcal{N}$

$\mathcal{N}$ $\mathcal{N}$ $\mathcal{N}$ $\mathcal{N}$ $\mathcal{N}$

$\mathcal{N}$ $\mathcal{N}$ $\mathcal{N}$ $\mathcal{N}$ $\mathcal{N}$ $\mathcal{N}$ $\mathcal{N}$

$\mathcal{N}$ $\mathcal{N}$ $\mathcal{N}$ $\mathcal{N}$ $\mathcal{N}$ $\mathcal{N}$ $\mathcal{N}$

n m m m

m m m m

n m m m m m m

m m m m m m m

A B C D E F G H I J K L M **N** O P Q R S T U V W X Y Z

n n n n n

n n

n n

n

m m m m m m

m m

m m

m

a b c d e f g h i j k l m n o p q r s t u v w x y z

Let's color!

Narwhal

Sight Words with N & n

no no no no no no

new new new new

not not not not

name name name name

Narwhal Narwhal

a b c d e f g h i j k l m n o p q r s t u v w x y z

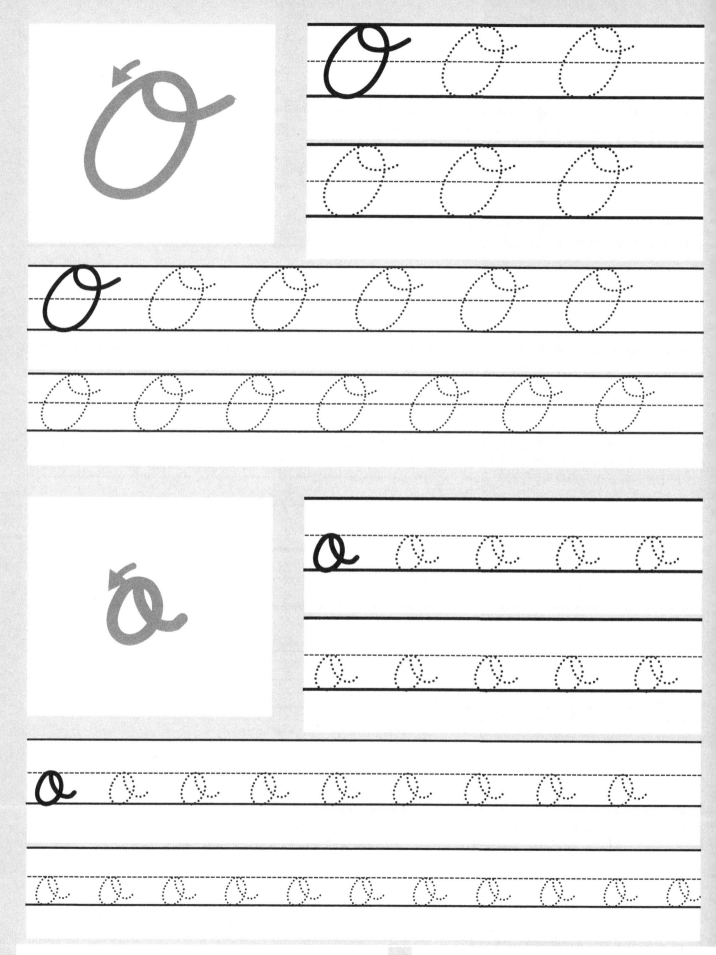

a b c d e f g h i j k l m n o p q r s t u v w x y z

Let's color!

Octopus

Sight Words with O & o

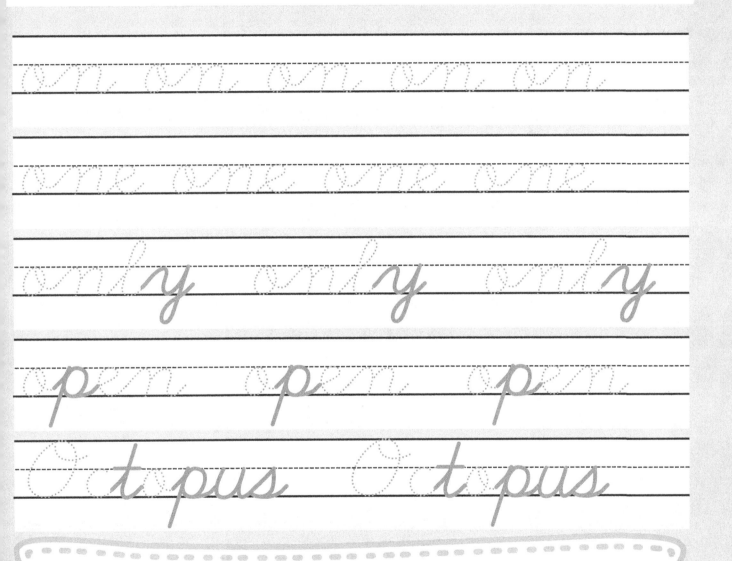

on on on on on on

one one one one one

only only only only

p p p p p

Octpus Octpus

Fun Fact:

Octopuses have three hearts and blue blood. They are also very intelligent and can solve puzzles.

a b c d e f g h i j k l m n o p q r s t u v w x y z

P P P P P P

P P P P P

P P P P P P P P P

P P P P P P P P P P

p p p p p

p p p p p

p p p p p p p p p p

p p p p p p p p p p p

a b c d e f g h i j k l m n o p q r s t u v w x y z

Let's color!

Penguin

Sight Words with P & p

people people people

pleas pleas pleas

put put put put put

play play play play play

Penguin Penguin Penguin

Fun Fact:

Penguins can't fly, but they are excellent swimmers. Some penguins can swim as fast as 15 miles per hour.

a b c d e f g h i j k l m n o p q r s t u v w x y z

2

2

q

q

a b c d e f g h i j k l m n o p q r s t u v w x y z

Let's color!

Quokka

Sight Words with
2 & q

quick quick quick

quiet quiet qui

queen queen qu

question question

Quokka Quokka

Fun Fact:

The quokka, a small marsupial from Australia, is
often called the "happiest animal" because of its
smiling face.

a b c d e f g h i j k l m n o p q r s t u v w x y z

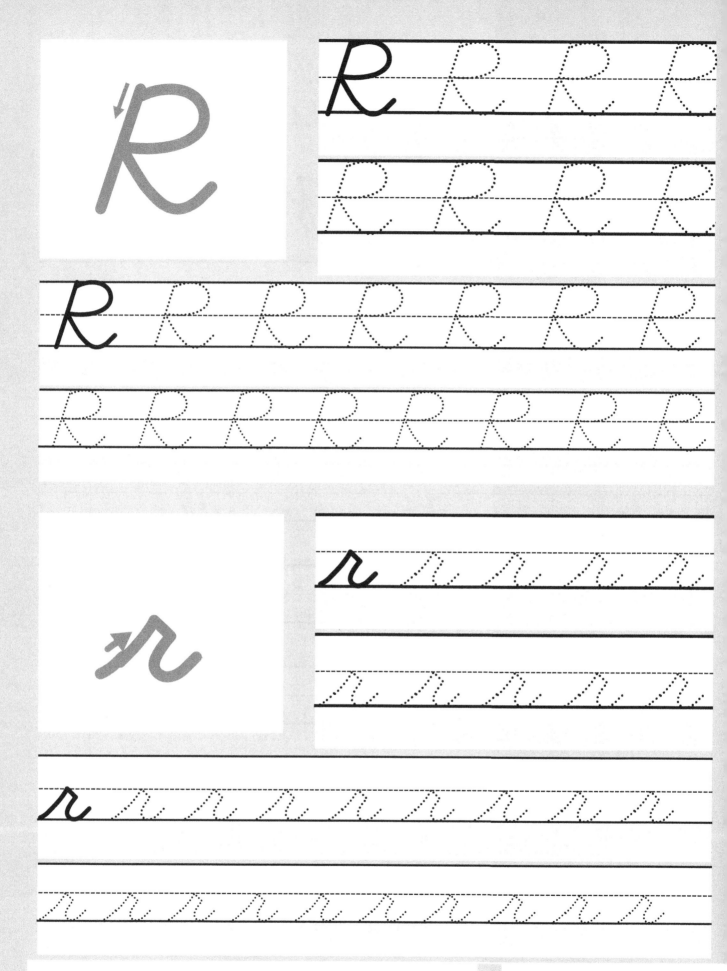

a b c d e f g h i j k l m n o p q r s t u v w x y z

Let's color!

Rabbit

Sight Words with R & r

red red red red red red

run run run run

really y really y

night night night night

Rabbit Rabbit

Fun Fact:

Rabbits have 360-degree vision, allowing them to see what's happening behind them without turning their heads.

a b c d e f g h i j k l m n o p q r s t u v w x y z

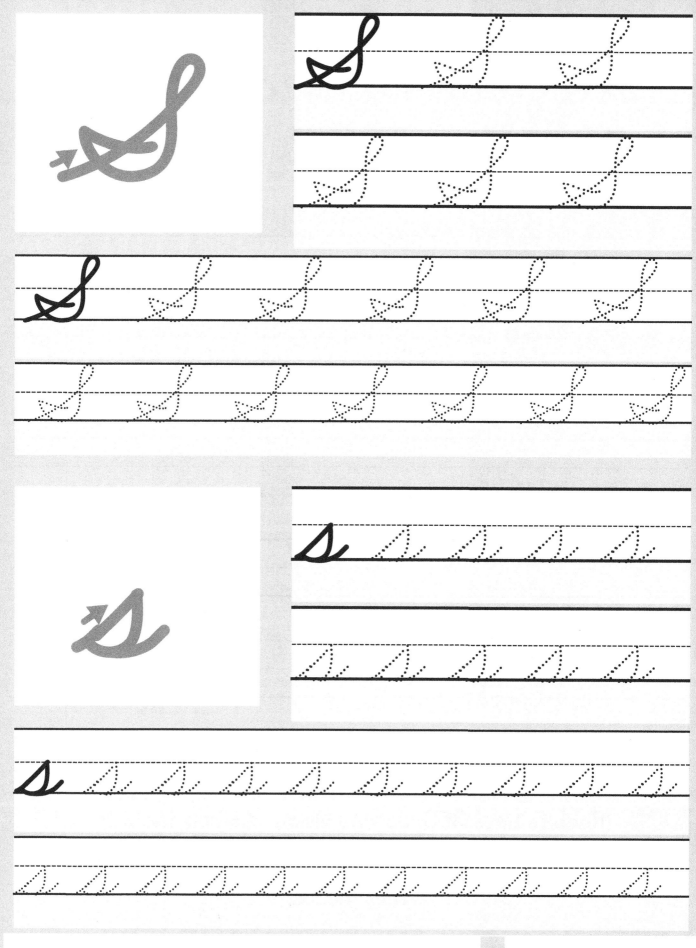

a b c d e f g h i j k l m n o p q r s t u v w x y z

Let's color!

Snake

Sight Words with
S & s

see

said

some

she

Snake

Fun Fact:
Snakes are fascinating reptiles that shed their skin several times a year. They do this to grow and to remove parasites. Some snakes, like the rattlesnake, have a rattle made of keratin (the same material as human nails) at the end of their tails to warn off predators.

a b c d e f g h i j k l m n o p q r s t u v w x y z

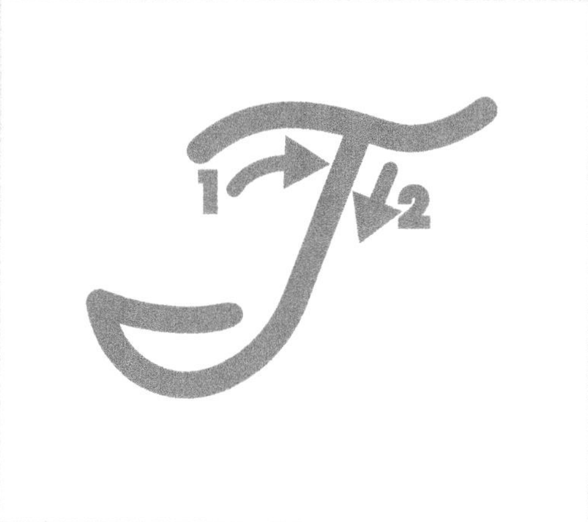

T T T

T T T

T T T T T T

T T T T T T

t t t t t

t t t t t

t t t t t t t t t t

t t t t t t t t t t t t t t

A B C D E F G H I J K L M N O P Q R S T U V W X Y Z

a b c d e f g h i j k l m n o p q r s t u v w x y z

Let's color!

Tiger

Sight Words with
T & t

the the the the the the

to to to to to to to to to

that that that that that

this this this this this

Tiger Tiger Tiger

Fun Fact:
Tigers have striped skin, not just striped fur. Each tiger's stripes are unique, like fingerprints.

a b c d e f g h i j k l m n o p q r s t u v w x y z

$\mathcal{U}$ $\mathcal{U}$ $\mathcal{U}$ $\mathcal{U}$ $\mathcal{U}$

$\mathcal{U}$ $\mathcal{U}$ $\mathcal{U}$ $\mathcal{U}$ $\mathcal{U}$

$\mathcal{U}$ $\mathcal{U}$ $\mathcal{U}$ $\mathcal{U}$ $\mathcal{U}$ $\mathcal{U}$ $\mathcal{U}$

$\mathcal{U}$ $\mathcal{U}$ $\mathcal{U}$ $\mathcal{U}$ $\mathcal{U}$ $\mathcal{U}$ $\mathcal{U}$ $\mathcal{U}$

u u u u u

u u u u u

u u u u u u u u u u u

A B C D E F G H I J K L M N O P Q R S T U V W X Y Z

a b c d e f g h i j k l m n o p q r s t u v w x y z

Let's color!

Urial

Sight Words with U & u

up up up up up up up

us us us us us us

under under under

until until until

Uriel Uriel Uriel

Fun Fact:
Urials are wild sheep found in Central Asia, known for their impressive curved horns. These horns can grow up to 3 feet long in males, and they use them to fight for dominance and mates.

a b c d e f g h i j k l m n o p q r s t u v w x y z

A B C D E F G H I J K L M N O P Q R S T U V W X Y Z

a b c d e f g h i j k l m n o p q r s t u v w x y z

Let's color!

Vampire Bat

Sight Words with
V & u

very very y very very y very very y

voice voice voice

visit visit visit

virus virus virus virus virus virus

Vampire Bat

Fun Fact:

Vampire bats are the only mammals that feed entirely on blood. They can locate their prey in total darkness using echolocation.

a b c d e f g h i j k l m n o p q r s t u v w x y z

abcdefghijklmnopqrstuvwxyz

Let's color!

Whale

Sight Words with W & w

we we we we we

what what what

when when when

who who who who

Whale Whale

a b c d e f g h i j k l m n o p q r s t u v w x y z

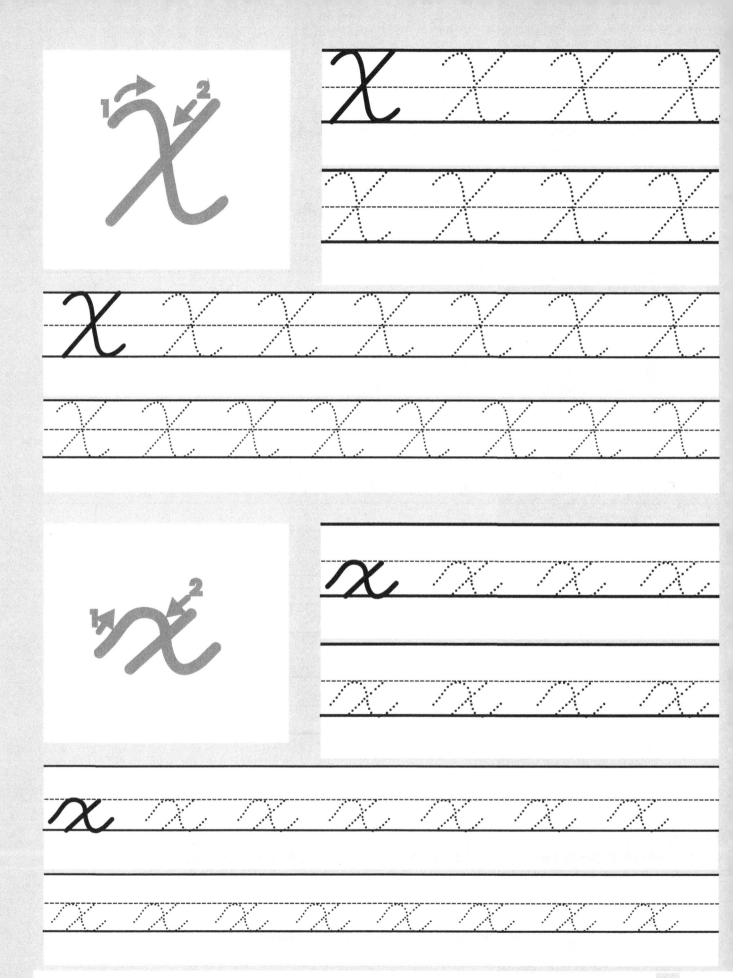

a b c d e f g h i j k l m n o p q r s t u v w x y z

Let's color!

Xerus

Sight Words with X & x

box box box box

six six six six six

mix mix mix

extra extra extra

Xerus Xerus Xerus

Fun Fact:
Xerus are African ground squirrels that live in burrows in the savannahs and deserts. They have bushy tails that they use as umbrellas to shade themselves from the hot sun.

a b c d e f g h i j k l m n o p q r s t u v w x y z

$$\mathcal{A} \; \mathcal{B} \; \mathcal{C} \; \mathcal{D} \; \mathcal{E} \; \mathcal{F} \; \mathcal{G} \; \mathcal{H} \; \mathcal{I} \; \mathcal{J} \; \mathcal{K} \; \mathcal{L} \; \mathcal{M} \; \mathcal{N} \; \mathcal{O} \; \mathcal{P} \; \mathcal{Q} \; \mathcal{R} \; \mathcal{S} \; \mathcal{T} \; \mathcal{U} \; \mathcal{V} \; \mathcal{W} \; \mathcal{X} \; \mathcal{Y} \; \mathcal{Z}$$

a b c d e f g h i j k l m n o p q r s t u v w x y z

Let's color!

Yak

Sight Words with Y & y

you you you you

yes yes yes yes yes

yellow yellow

your your your

Yak Yak Yak Yak

Fun Fact:

Yaks are large, long-haired animals found in the Himalayas. They can survive in extremely cold temperatures.

a b c d e f g h i j k l m n o p q r s t u v w x y z

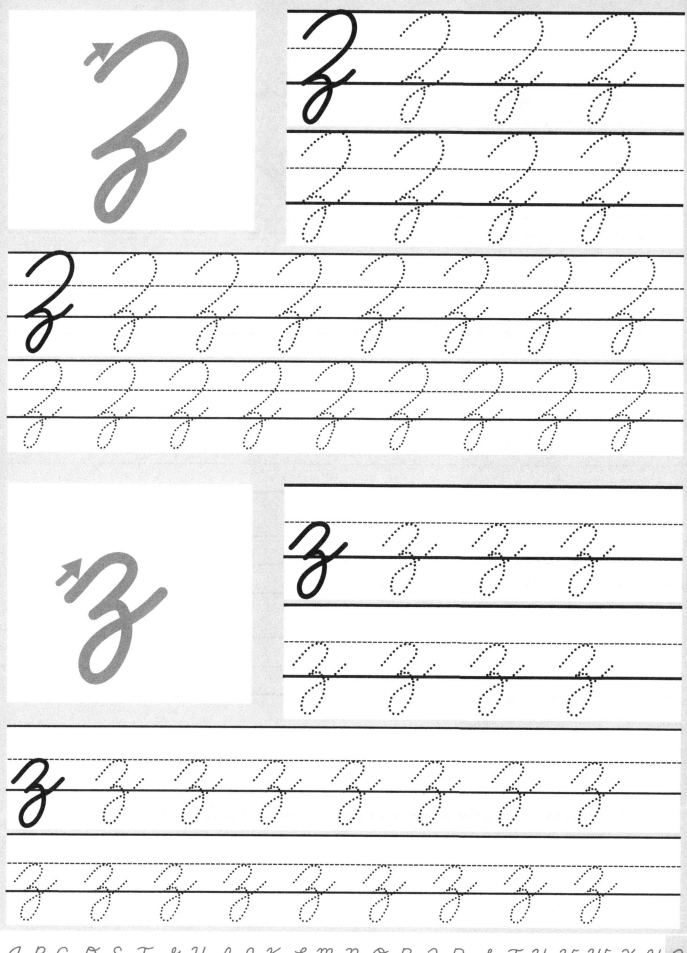

a b c d e f g h i j k l m n o p q r s t u v w x y z

Let's color!

Zebra

Sight Words with
Z & z

zoo zoo zoo zoo zoo

zip zip zip zip zip

zoo zoo zoo zoo

zigzag zigzag zigzag

zebra zebra zebra

Fun Fact:

Zebras' stripes are unique to each individual, much like human fingerprints. They help zebras recognize each other.

a b c d e f g h i j k l m n o p q r s t u v w x y z

Let's practice sentences!

You can do it.

You can do it.

Keep trying.

never give up.

Help others

whenever you can

You are amazing.

Dream big dreams

Kindness is cool.

IMPRINT

The author Andrea Lopez is represented by:

Andrea Schiffer
c/o COCENTER
Koppoldstr. 1
86551 Aichach
Germany

Email: andrea@lern.monster

ISBN: 979-8329273311
Year of Publication: 2024

Made in the USA
Las Vegas, NV
13 December 2024

13800866R00063